Master Your Money Mind:

Why Traditional Financial Advice is Holding You Back and How to Break Free

Mikey “Cap’n O’Shea” Miller

ISBN: 978-1-959555-72-8

DEDICATION

This book is dedicated to all the individuals who are tired of feeling overwhelmed and frustrated with their finances. To those who have struggled to make progress towards their financial goals despite following traditional financial advice.

I dedicate this book to you, because you inspired me to write it. Your struggles and challenges motivated me to find a better way to manage money, one that considers the complexities of our modern financial landscape and offers a personalized approach to achieving financial success.

May this book empower you to break free from the limitations of traditional financial advice and help you create a new relationship with money that empowers you to achieve the life you want.

CONTENTS

ACKNOWLEDGMENTS

I would like to express my deepest gratitude to everyone who has supported me throughout the writing of this book.

First and foremost, I want to thank my family and friends for their unwavering love and support. Their encouragement and motivation have been instrumental in helping me persevere through the challenges of writing a book.

I am grateful to my mentors for their guidance and insight throughout the editing process, which has helped me to refine my ideas and communicate them effectively to my readers.

I would also like to thank the experts and professionals in the financial industry who generously shared their knowledge and experiences with me. Their insights and perspectives have enriched the content of this book and made it a more valuable resource for readers.

Finally, I would like to express my appreciation to the readers of this book. Your interest in improving your financial well-being and breaking free from traditional financial advice has inspired me to write this book, and I hope that the information and strategies presented here will be of great help to you in achieving your financial goals.

Chapter 1 Introduction

Welcome to "Master Your Money Mind: Why Traditional Financial Advice is Holding You Back and How to Break Free."

Are you tired of following traditional financial advice that seems to leave you feeling more overwhelmed and frustrated? Do you feel like no matter how hard you try, you can't seem to get ahead financially? You're not alone. Many people struggle with managing their money and feeling like they're not making progress towards their financial goals.

The truth is, traditional financial advice is often outdated and doesn't take into account the complexities of our modern financial landscape. It's important to recognize that there's no one-size-fits-all solution when it comes to personal finance. Your financial situation is unique, and you need a personalized approach to managing your money.

That's where "Master Your Money Mind" comes in. This book is designed to help you break free from the limitations of traditional financial advice and take control of your finances. It will provide you with a new perspective on money and offer practical strategies to help you achieve financial success on your own terms.

In this book, you'll learn how to identify and overcome the limiting beliefs that are holding you back from reaching your financial goals. You'll discover how to cultivate a money mindset that empowers you to make smart financial decisions and achieve the life you want.

You'll also learn practical strategies for managing your money, including how to create a personalized financial plan that aligns with your goals and values, how to manage debt, and how to navigate life transitions that impact your finances.

"Master Your Money Mind" is not just another book about personal finance. It's a guide to help you transform your relationship with money and achieve financial freedom. It's time to break free from the limitations of traditional financial advice and create a financial plan that works for you.

2 The Psychology of Money

When it comes to managing our finances, it's not just about dollars and cents - it's also about mindset and behavior. The way we think about money, our beliefs and attitudes around it, and our financial habits all play a crucial role in our financial success. That's why understanding the psychology of money is so important.

The Role of Mindset in Financial Success

Have you ever made an impulse purchase and regretted it later? Or held onto a stock for too long despite evidence suggesting it was time to sell?
These are examples of how emotions can impact our financial decisions.

When it comes to money, we are often driven by our emotions, and this can lead to irrational decisions. Understanding our emotional relationship with money is the first step towards mastering our finances.

Our Beliefs About Money

Our beliefs about money are formed early in life and are influenced by our upbringing, culture, and social status. These beliefs can either help or hinder our financial success. For example, if you grew up in a family that struggled with money, you may have a scarcity mindset that makes it difficult to accumulate wealth. Alternatively, if you were raised in a family that valued financial stability, you may have a more positive relationship with money.

Many of us have heard the phrase "mind over matter," but when it comes to money, it's more like "mind over money." Our mindset plays a significant role in our financial success. A positive, growth-oriented mindset can help us overcome financial challenges, stay motivated, and ultimately achieve our financial goals.

On the other hand, a negative, scarcity-oriented mindset can hold us back and prevent us from reaching our financial potential. Beliefs like "I'll never be able to save enough money" or "I'm not good with money" can create a self-fulfilling prophecy, making it difficult to change our financial situation.

But the good news is that our mindset is not fixed. We can change our beliefs and attitudes about money, and in doing so, change our financial outcomes. The first step is recognizing that our mindset matters.

Identifying Limiting Beliefs and Behaviors Around Money

One of the keys to developing a healthy mindset around money is identifying and addressing any limiting beliefs or behaviors we may have. These can be beliefs like "money is the root of all evil," or behaviors like avoiding looking at our bank account balance.

To identify any limiting beliefs or behaviors around money, try journaling about your financial thoughts and feelings. Pay attention to any recurring patterns or themes that come up. Do you tend to feel anxious or stressed when thinking about money? Do you have a belief that you'll never be able to save enough? Once you've identified any limiting beliefs or behaviors, work on reframing them in a more positive and growth-oriented way.

Developing a Growth Mindset for Financial Success

A growth mindset is the belief that we can always improve and develop new skills. When it comes to money, a growth mindset means believing that we can improve our financial situation through learning and effort.

Here are some strategies for developing a growth mindset around money:

Focus on progress, not perfection. Celebrate small victories and acknowledge that financial progress takes time.

Embrace challenges. Financial challenges can be an opportunity to learn and grow. Instead of avoiding them, approach them with a positive attitude and a willingness to learn.

Learn from mistakes. We all make financial mistakes, but the key is to learn from them and use them as an opportunity to grow and improve.

Seek out education and resources. Developing a growth mindset means recognizing that we can always learn more about money and personal finance. Take advantage of resources like books, podcasts, and financial education programs.

The Psychology of Spending

Understanding our psychology around spending is also crucial to developing a healthy relationship with money. Our spending habits are often driven by our emotions and our beliefs about money.

For example, we may make an impulsive purchase to feel better after a stressful day at work, or we may believe that buying expensive things will make us feel more successful or important.

To develop a healthier relationship with spending, it's important to identify our emotional triggers and beliefs around money. Are we making purchases out of boredom, stress, or loneliness? Do we believe that material possessions will bring us happiness or status?

Once we've identified our emotional triggers and beliefs around spending, we can work on developing healthier habits. This might include creating a budget, practicing mindful spending, or seeking out support from friends or professionals.
Additionally, it's important to recognize the influence of societal

and cultural factors on our relationship with money. For example, some cultures emphasize the importance of saving money for the future while others prioritize spending money on experiences in the present. Understanding these cultural and societal influences can help us identify any limiting beliefs or biases we may hold about money and work towards developing a healthier relationship with it.

The Role of Emotions in Our Financial Decisions

It's common to think of money as a purely rational concept. However, the truth is that emotions play a significant role in our financial decisions. Many of our financial decisions are driven by our emotions, whether we realize it or not.

For example, fear is a common emotion that can influence our financial decisions. When the stock market experiences a downturn, many investors may feel fearful and decide to sell their investments. This decision is often driven by a desire to avoid potential losses, even if it means missing out on potential gains in the future.

On the other hand, greed is another emotion that can impact our financial decisions. When the market is performing well, it's easy to become overconfident and make risky investments in the hopes of making a quick profit. However, these decisions are often driven by greed and can lead to significant financial losses in the long run.

Other emotions that can impact our financial decisions include anxiety, shame, and guilt. These emotions may cause us to avoid making financial decisions altogether or make decisions that are not in our best interest.

Developing a Healthy Relationship with Money

To develop a healthy relationship with money, it's important to understand the role of emotions in our financial decisions and take steps to manage them. Here are a few tips to get started:

Identify your emotional triggers: Take some time to reflect on your past financial decisions and identify any emotions that may have influenced them. For example, did fear drive you to sell your investments during a
market downturn? Did greed lead you to make a risky investment?

Practice mindfulness: Mindfulness can be a helpful tool for managing emotions and developing a healthier relationship with money. When you feel an emotional urge to make a financial decision, take a moment to pause and observe your thoughts and feelings. This can help you make a more rational decision based on your financial goals and values.

My favorite mindfullness practice I have been using daily is called The Tapping Solution
https://www.thetappingsolution.com/

Set realistic financial goals: Setting realistic financial goals can help you make more informed decisions based on your priorities and values. For example, if your goal is to save money for retirement, you may be less likely to make impulsive purchases that could impact your long-term savings.

Practice self-compassion: It's important to remember that everyone makes financial mistakes from time to time. Instead of beating yourself up over past mistakes, practice self-compassion and focus on what you can do to make positive changes moving forward.

Seek support: If you're struggling with managing your emotions around money, consider seeking support from a financial advisor, therapist, or trusted friend or family member. They can provide guidance and support as you work towards developing a healthier relationship with money.

Conclusion

The psychology of money is a complex and often overlooked topic in personal finance. However, understanding the role of emotions in our financial decisions and taking steps to manage them can help us develop a healthier relationship with money and make more informed financial decisions based on our priorities and values. By identifying our emotional triggers, practicing mindfulness, setting realistic financial goals, practicing self-compassion, and seeking support when needed, we can break free from limiting beliefs and behaviors and master our money mind.

If you're like most people, you've probably been following traditional financial advice for years. Maybe you've been following the advice of your parents, your friends, or your financial advisor. You've been told to save for retirement, invest in stocks and bonds, and avoid debt at all costs. But have you ever stopped to think about whether this advice is really working for you?

Chapter 2 Recommended Book Resources:

(If you click on one of the links and purchase I will receive an affiliate commission)

"The Millionaire Mind" by Thomas J. Stanley - This book explores the habits, attitudes, and beliefs of millionaires and how they differ from those of the general population.

"Think and Grow Rich" by Napoleon Hill - This classic book emphasizes the importance of positive thinking and visualization in achieving financial success.

"The Psychology of Money" by Morgan Housel - This book explores the intersection of psychology and finance and how our beliefs and behaviors around money impact our financial outcomes.

"The Power of Positive Thinking" by Norman Vincent Peale - This book focuses on the role of positive thinking and attitude in achieving success in all areas of life, including finance.

In the next chapter, we'll take a closer look at the problem with traditional financial advice and why it may be holding you back from achieving your financial goals.

Chapter 3 The Problem with Traditional Financial Advice

The Problem with One-Size-Fits-All Advice

One of the biggest problems with traditional financial advice is that it's often one-size-fits-all. Advisors and experts often give the same advice to everyone, regardless of their unique financial situation, goals, and risk tolerance. This can lead to people investing in assets that aren't right for them or taking on debt that they can't handle.

For example, let's say that you've been told to invest heavily in the stock market. While this may be a good strategy for some people, it may not be the best choice for you. Perhaps you have a low risk tolerance and would feel more comfortable investing in bonds or real estate. If you follow the one-size-fits-all advice of your financial advisor, you may end up investing in stocks that make you feel uneasy and anxious.

The Problem with Overemphasizing Saving

Another problem with traditional financial advice is that it often overemphasizes saving and underemphasizes earning. While saving is certainly important, it's only half of the equation. If you're not earning enough money to meet your financial goals, no amount of saving will get you there.

This overemphasis on saving can also lead to people becoming overly frugal and not enjoying their lives. They may avoid spending money on things that bring them joy or invest too conservatively out of fear of losing their hard-earned savings.

The Problem with Fear-Based Advice

Lastly, traditional financial advice is often fear-based. Advisors and experts may focus on worst-case scenarios and the potential for financial loss, which can create a sense of panic and anxiety in people. This fear-based approach can lead to people making impulsive decisions, such as selling stocks during a market downturn or avoiding investing altogether.

Additionally, fear-based advice can prevent people from taking calculated risks that could lead to higher returns. For example, an advisor may discourage you from investing in a new and innovative company because of the perceived risk. However, by avoiding these opportunities, you may miss out on potentially high returns.

Breaking Free from Traditional Financial Advice

Now that we've identified the problems with traditional financial advice, it's time to start thinking about how to break free from it. Here are some strategies to help you do just that:

Work with a Financial Coach
Instead of relying on a traditional financial advisor, consider working with a financial coach. A coach can help you create a customized financial plan that takes into account your unique goals, risk tolerance, and lifestyle. They can also help you stay accountable and make adjustments to your plan as needed.

Visit Dave Ramsey's Endorsed Local Providers to find a financial coach that know their job is "to serve, not sell"

Emphasize Earning, Not Just Saving
Remember that earning is just as important as saving when it comes to achieving your financial goals. Instead of solely focusing on saving money, think about ways to increase your income. This could include starting a side business, negotiating a raise, or investing in yourself through education and training.

Focus on Long-Term Goals
Don't let fear-based advice derail your long-term financial goals. Instead, focus on your long-term vision and stay committed to your plan, even during market downturns or economic uncertainty.

Take Calculated Risks
As we delve further into the world of traditional financial advice, we come across another problem: the one-size-fits-all approach.

Many financial advisors will tell you that there are certain rules that apply to everyone when it comes to managing money. For example, they might say that you should always save 10% of your income, or that you should never have more than 30% of your income going towards housing expenses.

While these rules may work for some people, they do not work for everyone. Everyone has their own unique financial situation, and what works for one person may not work for another. This is why it is important to break free from traditional financial advice and instead focus on what works best for you.

Additionally, traditional financial advice often fails to take into account the emotional and psychological aspects of money. Money is not just a practical matter – it also has deep emotional roots that can influence our behavior.

For example, someone who grew up in a household where money was always tight may have a deeply ingrained fear of running out of money, which can lead them to hoard their savings and avoid taking risks. On the other hand, someone who grew up with plenty of money may have a sense of entitlement and spend beyond their means.

Traditional financial advice often fails to recognize these emotional factors, and instead focuses solely on the practical aspects of managing money. This can lead to a disconnect between what people are told they should do with their money and what they actually do.

To truly master your money mind, you need to take a holistic approach that takes into account both the practical and emotional aspects of money. This means breaking free from traditional financial advice and instead focusing on what works best for you, as an individual.

Chapter 3 Recommended Book Resources:

(If you click on one of the links and purchase I will receive an affiliate commission)

"The Simple Path to Wealth" by JL Collins - This book challenges traditional financial advice and promotes a simple, DIY approach to investing.

"Your Money or Your Life" by Vicki Robin and Joe Dominguez - This book offers a holistic approach to personal finance, emphasizing the importance of aligning your spending and saving habits with your values and goals

In the following chapters, we will explore the many ways in which traditional financial advice is holding you back, and provide you with the tools and strategies you need to break free and achieve financial success on your own terms.

Chapter 4 The Power of Habits: How Habits Influence Financial Behavior

We all have habits – both good and bad – that shape our behavior and influence our daily lives. When it comes to money, our habits can have a profound impact on our financial health and well-being.

In fact, research has shown that as much as 40% of our daily actions are based on habits rather than conscious decisions. This means that the financial habits we form can have a significant impact on our financial outcomes.

So, how do habits influence financial behavior? The answer lies in the way our brains process information and make decisions. Habits are deeply ingrained patterns of behavior that are stored in our subconscious minds. When we encounter a situation that triggers a particular habit, our brains automatically revert to that behavior without us even thinking about it.

This can be both a blessing and a curse when it comes to money. On the one hand, good financial habits – like regularly saving a portion of your income or paying off credit card balances in full each month – can help you achieve long-term financial success. On the other hand, bad financial habits – like overspending or failing to save for retirement – can lead to financial stress and instability.

Creating and sticking to healthy financial habits is key to achieving financial success. Here are some tips to help you do just that:

Set clear financial goals: Habits are much easier to form and stick to when they are aligned with a clear goal. Whether it's saving for a down payment on a house or paying off debt, having a specific goal in mind can help you stay motivated and focused.

Make small changes: Trying to overhaul your entire financial life at once is overwhelming and can lead to burnout. Instead, focus on making small, incremental changes that gradually build up to a bigger overall improvement.

Automate your finances: Automation is a powerful tool for creating and sticking to good financial habits. Set up automatic transfers to savings accounts, automate bill payments, and use budgeting apps to help you stay on track.

Practice mindfulness: Mindfulness is the practice of being present in the moment and aware of your thoughts and emotions. By practicing mindfulness, you can become more aware of your financial habits and make intentional decisions about how you want to behave with money.

Identifying and breaking bad financial habits is equally important for achieving financial success. Here are some tips to help you do just that:

Identify your triggers: Habits are often triggered by specific situations or emotions. For example, you may have a habit of overspending when you're feeling stressed or anxious. By identifying your triggers, you can start to develop strategies for breaking the habit.

Replace bad habits with good ones: Breaking a bad habit is much easier when you replace it with a good one. For example, if you have a habit of overspending when you're feeling down, try going for a walk or calling a friend instead.

Use visualization techniques: Visualization is a powerful tool for breaking bad habits. Close your eyes and visualize yourself behaving in a different way when faced with your trigger situation. The more vividly you can imagine the new behavior, the easier it will be to make the change in real life.

Track your progress: Habits take time to form, and breaking bad habits can be a long process. Keep track of your progress and celebrate small victories along the way to stay motivated

Get my favorite 66 Day Challenge™ Calendar habit tracker from the One Thing Resource Page.

In conclusion, the power of habits cannot be underestimated when it comes to financial behavior. By creating and sticking to healthy financial habits, and identifying and breaking bad ones, you can achieve long-term financial success and stability.

To further illustrate the power of habits in achieving financial goals, let's take a closer look at a few examples.

One of the most common financial goals is saving for retirement. Many people dream of being able to retire comfortably, but struggle to put away enough money to make it a reality. However, by creating and sticking to healthy financial habits, this goal can become much more achievable. For example, making a habit of automatically contributing a certain percentage of each paycheck to a retirement account, such as a 401(k) or IRA, can help ensure that retirement savings grow steadily over time. This simple habit can make a significant difference in the long run.

On the other hand, bad financial habits can hinder progress toward financial goals. For example, overspending can be a difficult habit to break. People who frequently make impulse purchases or habitually spend more than they earn often find themselves struggling to make ends meet, let alone save for the future. Breaking this habit requires a concerted effort, but it is possible. Some strategies for overcoming overspending habits include creating and sticking to a budget, avoiding temptation (such as by unsubscribing from retailer emails or avoiding online shopping), and seeking support from a financial advisor or accountability partner.

Ultimately, the power of habits lies in their ability to shape our actions and behaviors over time. By identifying and cultivating healthy financial habits, and breaking bad ones, anyone can make progress toward their financial goals. It takes time and effort, but the rewards can be significant.

Chapter 4 Recommended Book Resources:

(If you click on one of the links and purchase I will receive an affiliate commission)

"Mindset: The New Psychology of Success" by Carol Dweck - This book explores the concept of fixed and growth mindsets and how they impact our ability to learn, grow, and achieve our goals.

"The Power of Now" by Eckhart Tolle - This book focuses on the importance of being present in the moment and how our thoughts and beliefs can limit our ability to experience inner peace and happiness.

"Breaking the Habit of Being Yourself: How to Lose Your Mind and Create a New One" by Joe Dispenza - This book provides insights into how the mind works and offers practical strategies for overcoming limiting beliefs and behaviors.

"The Gifts of Imperfection: Let Go of Who You Think You're Supposed to Be and Embrace Who You Are" by Brené Brown - This book encourages readers to let go of perfectionism and embrace vulnerability as a means

Atomic Habits an Easy & Proven Way to Build Good Habits and Break Bad Ones James Clear This book presents a simple, evidence-based approach to building good habits and breaking bad ones. It provides practical tips for making small changes that can lead to big results over time.

"The Power of Habit: Why We Do What We Do in Life and Business" by Charles Duhigg This book examines the science of habits and how they shape our lives, both personally and professionally. It provides actionable advice for breaking bad habits and building good ones.

Chapter 5: Money and Emotion

Money and emotions have an intertwined relationship. How we feel about money affects how we manage and use it. Sometimes, our emotions can take over, leading to irrational financial decisions. In this chapter, we will explore the emotional connection to money and provide strategies for managing them.

Understanding the Emotional Connection to Money

We all have emotional connections to money that are rooted in our upbringing, culture, and experiences. Our emotions can range from positive feelings such as happiness, security, and pride to negative feelings such as fear, anxiety, and shame. Understanding these emotional connections is crucial to taking control of our financial lives.

For some, money represents security and stability. They may feel a sense of comfort and safety when they have a significant amount of money in the bank. On the other hand, for others, money may represent freedom and flexibility. They may feel empowered when they have the financial resources to do what they want, when they want.

However, money can also be a source of stress and anxiety. Financial worries can keep us up at night and cause physical and emotional distress. Sometimes, our emotions can lead to irrational financial decisions, such as making impulsive purchases or avoiding financial decisions altogether.

How Emotions Can Affect Financial Decision-Making

Our emotions can influence how we make financial decisions. For example, fear of missing out (FOMO) can lead us to invest in speculative investments or take on too much debt. Conversely, when we are feeling overly optimistic, we may take on too much risk and invest in inappropriate assets.

Research has shown that emotions such as anger, anxiety, and sadness can lead to impulsive financial decisions. When we are feeling these emotions, we tend to focus on immediate gratification rather than long-term goals. It's important to be aware of these emotional triggers and make decisions based on our financial goals and values.

Strategies for Managing Emotions Around Money

Managing our emotions around money is critical to making sound financial decisions. Here are some strategies to help manage your emotions.

Identify Your Triggers - Identify the situations or events that trigger negative emotions around money. Understanding what triggers your emotions can help you develop strategies to manage them.

Create a Budget - A budget can help you gain control over your finances and reduce financial stress. By creating a spending plan, you can identify areas where you may be overspending and make adjustments accordingly.

Practice Mindfulness - Mindfulness can help you become more aware of your emotions and reduce impulsive financial decisions. By being present in the moment, you can focus on your financial goals and values.

Seek Professional Help - If you're struggling with managing your emotions around money, consider seeking professional help. A financial therapist can help you identify and work through emotional barriers to financial success.

To find a financial therapist visit
https://financialtherapyassociation.org/find-a-financial-therapist/

In this chapter, we explored the emotional connection to money and how our emotions can affect financial decision-making. By understanding our emotional triggers and developing strategies to manage them, we can take control of our financial lives. Remember, money is a tool, and our emotions should not control how we use it. By taking a mindful and intentional approach to our finances, we can achieve our financial goals and live a fulfilling life.

Chapter 5 Recommended Book Resources:

(If you click on one of the links and purchase I will receive an affiliate commission)

"Your Money and Your Brain" by Jason Zweig - This book explores the connection between brain chemistry and financial decision-making, providing insights into how emotions can influence our financial choices.

"Mind Over Money: The Psychology of Money and How to Use It Better" by Claudia Hammond - This book delves into the psychology behind our financial choices and provides practical tips for managing our money and emotions.

"Emotional Agility: Get Unstuck, Embrace Change, and Thrive in Work and Life" by Susan David - Although not specifically about money, this book provides insights into how to better understand and manage our emotions in all aspects of life, which can be applied to financial decision-making.

"The Behavioral Investor" by Daniel Crosby - This book explores the intersection of psychology and finance, providing insights into the emotional and cognitive biases that can impact our financial choices.

"Money, A Love Story: Untangle Your Financial Woes and Create the Life You Really Want" by Kate Northrup - This book focuses on the emotional relationship that we have with money, and provides strategies for transforming negative money beliefs and behaviors.

Chapter 6 Overcoming Financial Limitations

Many people struggle with financial limitations, whether it be living paycheck to paycheck, having a mountain of debt, or feeling like they'll never have enough money to achieve their goals. It's a common struggle, but it's important to know that there are ways to overcome these limitations and achieve financial freedom. In this chapter, we'll discuss several strategies for overcoming financial limitations and creating a brighter financial future.

Face the Reality of Your Situation

The first step in overcoming financial limitations is to face the reality of your situation. It can be tempting to avoid looking at your finances, but the longer you ignore them, the worse they'll become. Take a deep breath and look at your bank statements, credit card bills, and any other financial documents you've been avoiding. Make a list of all your debts, including balances and interest rates. It may be overwhelming, but knowing where you stand is essential to creating a plan to overcome your financial limitations.

If would like more information about how I paid off $20,000 of credit card debt in just 2 years, instead of 8-10 for half the amount visit https://www.nationaldebtrelief.com/howitworks/

Set Realistic Goals

Once you know where you stand financially, it's time to set some goals. Goals are important because they give you something to work towards and help you stay motivated. However, it's important to set realistic goals. If you're drowning in debt, your goal shouldn't be to become a millionaire overnight. Instead, set small, achievable goals, like paying off one credit card or saving $500 in an emergency fund. Celebrate each small win, and use them as motivation to keep going.

Create a Budget

One of the most important steps in overcoming financial limitations is creating a budget. A budget is simply a plan for how you'll spend your money. Start by tracking your expenses for a month, and then categorize them into fixed expenses (like rent or mortgage payments), variable expenses (like groceries and entertainment), and debt payments. Once you know where your money is going, you can create a plan for how to allocate it more effectively. Make sure to include a line item for savings, no matter how small the amount may be.

My favorite budgeting tool is from Dave Ramsey called Every Dollar

Reduce Your Debt

Debt is one of the biggest financial limitations for many people. If you're carrying a lot of debt, it can feel like you'll never be able to get out from under it. However, there are several strategies for reducing your debt. One approach is to focus on paying off the debt with the highest interest rate first, while making minimum payments on the rest. Another approach is to consolidate your debt into a single loan with a lower interest rate. This can simplify your payments and help you pay off your debt more quickly.

If you would like to learn the difference between paying off debt based on the highest interest, compared to paying off debt with the lowest interest consider reading the following Forbes article by Robin Saks Frankel

Debt Snowball Vs. Debt Avalanche: The Best Way To Pay Off Credit Card Debt

Increase Your Income

Increasing your income is another way to overcome financial limitations. Look for opportunities to increase your income, whether it be through a promotion at work, starting a side hustle, or taking on freelance work. You may also be able to negotiate a higher salary or hourly rate. Every little bit helps, and increasing your income can give you more flexibility in your budget and help you achieve your financial goals more quickly.

Cut Your Expenses

In addition to increasing your income, cutting your expenses can also help you overcome financial limitations. Look for ways to reduce your fixed expenses, such as by refinancing your mortgage or negotiating lower rates on your bills. You can also cut back on your variable expenses by finding ways to save on groceries, entertainment, and other non-essential expenses. It may take some creativity and sacrifice, but every dollar you save can help you achieve your financial goals more quickly.

I recommend TRIM if you are looking for a way to save on expenses like their 3 million customers who have saved over $86 million in unnecessary expenses.

Seek Professional Help

If you're struggling to overcome your financial limitations on your own, don't be afraid to seek professional help. A financial advisor can help you create a personalized plan for achieving your financial goals, and a credit counselor can help you develop a plan for paying off your debt.

Another way to overcome financial limitations is to develop a growth mindset. This is a belief system that emphasizes the power of effort, learning, and resilience in achieving success. People with a growth mindset understand that their abilities and intelligence can be developed through dedication and hard work. This perspective can be particularly helpful when it comes to money because it can help you see financial setbacks as opportunities for growth and learning.

Another important aspect of overcoming financial limitations is to find ways to increase your income. This may involve pursuing a new job, taking on a side gig, or starting your own business. While increasing your income is not always easy, it is an important step in building financial stability and freedom. Remember that small changes can add up over time, so don't be discouraged if your efforts do not produce immediate results. Consistency is key, and if you stay focused on your goals and take consistent action, you will eventually achieve the financial success you desire.

Finally, it is important to remember that financial limitations are not just about money. They can also be related to mindset, habits, and values. For example, if you have a negative relationship with money, or if you have habits that are holding you back, such as overspending or not saving enough, these issues need to be addressed in order to achieve financial freedom. Additionally, your values and priorities play a crucial role in determining how you use your money. By taking the time to reflect on your values and goals, you can create a financial plan that aligns with your priorities and helps you achieve the life you want.

In conclusion, overcoming financial limitations is a process that requires effort, dedication, and a willingness to learn and grow. By taking a holistic approach to your finances, including developing a growth mindset, finding ways to increase your income, and aligning your financial plan with your values, you can break free from financial constraints and achieve the financial success and freedom you desire. Remember that small steps can lead to big changes, and that it is never too late to start taking control of your financial future.

Chapter 6 Recommended Book Resources

(If you click on one of the links and purchase I will receive an affiliate commission)

"Rich Dad Poor Dad" by Robert Kiyosaki is a personal finance book that emphasizes the importance of financial education, investing, and entrepreneurship. The author shares his personal story of growing up with two different father figures - his biological father (poor dad) and his best friend's father (rich dad). The book highlights the different financial philosophies of these two individuals and how their beliefs and actions shaped their financial outcomes.

"Cash Flow Quadrant" by Robert Kiyosaki is a follow-up book to "Rich Dad Poor Dad" and focuses on the four different ways people earn money: as employees, self-employed individuals, business owners, or investors. Kiyosaki argues that people who want to achieve financial independence need to move from the left side of the cash flow quadrant (employee or self-employed) to the right side (business owner or investor).

"The Total Money Makeover" by Dave Ramsey is a personal finance book that provides a step-by-step plan for people to get out of debt and build wealth. The book focuses on seven "baby steps" that individuals can take to achieve financial freedom, including saving an emergency fund, paying off debt, and investing for retirement. Ramsey's approach emphasizes the importance of living below one's means and avoiding debt at all costs.

Chapter 7 Building Wealth

Building wealth is a key component of achieving financial freedom.

However, the process of accumulating wealth can seem overwhelming and daunting. In this chapter, we'll explore practical strategies and techniques that can help you build wealth and achieve your financial goals.

One of the first steps in building wealth is to develop a mindset that is focused on long-term goals and delayed gratification. This means being willing to make sacrifices and trade-offs in the present in order to achieve greater financial security and freedom in the future.

One of the most important things you can do to build wealth is to develop a plan for your finances. This should include setting clear financial goals, creating a budget that allows you to live within your means, and establishing a savings plan that enables you to save consistently over time.

Investing is another key element of building wealth. By investing your money wisely, you can potentially earn a higher rate of return than you would by simply saving your money in a bank account. However, investing also involves risk, and it's important to educate yourself about different types of investments and the associated risks before putting your money on the line.

Real estate is one investment option that has the potential to generate significant wealth over time. Whether you're interested in buying and holding rental properties or flipping houses for a profit, real estate can be a great way to build wealth and generate passive income.

Another way to build wealth is to start a business. Entrepreneurship can be a challenging and risky path, but it also offers the potential for significant financial rewards. By identifying a need in the market and developing a product or service that meets that need, you can create a successful business that generates wealth and provides you with financial freedom.

One of the most important things to keep in mind when building wealth is to avoid taking on too much debt. While some types of debt, such as a mortgage or student loans, may be necessary to achieve your financial goals, it's important to avoid high-interest debt like credit card debt that can quickly spiral out of control and derail your efforts to build wealth.

In addition to avoiding debt, it's important to focus on reducing your expenses and living below your means. By living frugally and making conscious choices about how you spend your money, you can free up more funds to invest in wealth-building opportunities.

In one of my trainings I took, the entrepreneur stated that there are only three things you need to run a successful business.

#1) A way to attract customers/clients

#2) A way to keep those customers/clients engaged so they continue working with you.

#3) Keep your net income above your expenses.

One effective strategy for building wealth is to invest in assets that appreciate over time. For example, real estate is a popular investment choice for many people because it tends to increase in value over time. By purchasing a property and renting it out, you can generate passive income and benefit from potential appreciation in the value of the property. Similarly, investing in stocks and mutual funds can provide long-term growth and increase your net worth over time.

Another strategy for managing your expenses is to avoid debt whenever possible and pay off existing debt as quickly as possible. High-interest debt like credit card balances and personal loans can quickly accumulate and lead to financial stress. By prioritizing debt repayment and avoiding taking on additional debt, you can free up more of your income to invest and build wealth over time.

Finally, building wealth requires patience and discipline. It's important to set realistic goals and create a long-term plan for achieving them. This may involve making sacrifices in the short-term in order to achieve long-term financial success. It's also important to avoid chasing get-rich-quick schemes or making impulsive investment decisions. Instead, focus on building a solid foundation of financial stability and consistently working towards your goals.

In conclusion, building wealth is a process that requires a combination of investing, entrepreneurship, careful expense management, and patience. By creating a long-term plan and consistently working towards your goals, you can achieve financial success and create a more secure future for yourself and your family.

Chapter 7 Recommended Book Resources:

(If you click on one of the links and purchase I will receive an affiliate commission)

Start Late, Finish Rich: A No-Fail Plan for Achieving Financial Freedom at Any Age by David Bach In a swift, motivating read, David Bach gives you step-by-step instructions, worksheets, phone numbers, and website addresses—everything you need to put your "Start Late" plan into place right away. You will learn that even if you're buried in debt, there's still hope. You can spend less, save more, and make more—and it doesn't have to hurt. With America's best-loved money coach at your side, it's never too late to change your financial destiny.

"The Automatic Millionaire" by David Bach is a personal finance book that emphasizes the importance of automating one's savings and investment contributions to achieve financial independence. Bach argues that by setting up automatic contributions to retirement accounts and other investment vehicles, individuals can save and invest without having to think about it. The book also stresses the importance of living below one's means and avoiding unnecessary expenses.

"The 4-Hour Work Week" by Timothy Ferriss: This book presents a new perspective on wealth-building, focusing on lifestyle design, productivity, and entrepreneurship.

"The Richest Man in Babylon" by George S. Clason - This book offers timeless financial advice through parables set in ancient Babylon, emphasizing the importance of disciplined saving and investing.

"The ABCs of Real Estate Investing" by Ken McElroy - This book covers the basics of real estate investing, including finding deals, evaluating properties, financing, and managing rental properties. McElroy also includes case studies and real-world examples.

"The Millionaire Real Estate Investor" by Gary Keller, Dave Jenks, and Jay Papasan - This book provides practical advice on how to become a successful real estate investor, covering topics such as finding investment properties, financing deals, and building a portfolio.

Chapter 8 Managing Debt

Debt can be a significant financial burden for many individuals, and if left unmanaged, it can have long-term negative impacts on personal finances. In this chapter, we'll discuss various strategies for managing debt, including understanding the types of debt, creating a repayment plan, and working with financial professionals to address debt.

Understanding the Types of Debt

Before we can effectively manage our debt, it's essential to understand the different types of debt that we may have. Some common forms of debt include credit card debt, student loans, mortgages, car loans, and personal loans. Each type of debt may have different interest rates, repayment terms, and consequences for missed payments. It's essential to understand the specifics of each type of debt to create a comprehensive plan for managing debt.

Creating a Repayment Plan

One effective way to manage debt is to create a repayment plan. A repayment plan involves developing a schedule for paying off debts over time, which can help individuals stay on track with their payments and reduce interest charges. Here are some strategies for creating a repayment plan:

Prioritize High-Interest Debt

Begin by focusing on high-interest debts, such as credit card debt or personal loans. These types of debts can quickly spiral out of control, and the longer they go unpaid, the more interest will accrue.

Consider a Balance Transfer

For individuals with high-interest credit card debt, a balance transfer may be an effective option. A balance transfer involves moving high-interest credit card debt to a credit card with a lower interest rate, which can help reduce interest charges and make payments more manageable.

Negotiate with Lenders

In some cases, it may be possible to negotiate with lenders to reduce interest rates or payment amounts. This may be particularly effective for individuals with high levels of debt who are struggling to make payments.

Create a Budget

Creating a budget can help individuals identify areas where they can reduce expenses and redirect funds towards debt repayment. By tracking income and expenses, individuals can develop a realistic plan for paying off debt over time.

Working with Financial Professionals

In some cases, managing debt may require the assistance of financial professionals, such as financial advisors or credit counselors. These professionals can provide guidance on debt management strategies, negotiate with lenders on behalf of clients, and help individuals create a comprehensive plan for managing debt. Here are some ways financial professionals can help with managing debt:

Credit Counseling

Credit counseling is a service provided by nonprofit organizations that can help individuals develop a debt management plan. Credit counselors can work with individuals to negotiate with lenders, reduce interest rates, and create a budget for paying off debt.

Financial Advisors

Financial advisors can help individuals develop a long-term financial plan that includes debt management strategies. By working with a financial advisor, individuals can receive guidance on investing, retirement planning, and other aspects of personal finance that can impact debt management.

Debt Consolidation

Debt consolidation involves taking out a new loan to pay off multiple debts. This strategy can be effective for individuals with high levels of debt, as it can simplify payments and reduce interest charges. Financial professionals can help individuals identify the best debt consolidation options for their specific needs.

Conclusion

Managing debt is an essential aspect of personal finance, and it requires careful planning and diligence. By understanding the types of debt, creating a repayment plan, and working with financial professionals, individuals can take control of their debt and reduce the long-term negative impacts of financial stress. With effective debt management strategies in place, individuals can focus on building wealth and achieving their long-term financial goals.

Chapter 8 Recommended Book Resources:

(If you click on one of the links and purchase I will receive an affiliate commission)

"Debt-Free Forever: Take Control of Your Money and Your Life" by Gail Vaz-Oxlade - This book offers practical advice for eliminating debt and creating a sustainable financial plan. Vaz-Oxlade emphasizes the importance of understanding your spending habits and making changes to live within your means.

"The Debt Escape Plan: How to Free Yourself From Credit Card Balances, Boost Your Credit Score, and Live Debt-Free" by Beverly

Harzog - This book offers a comprehensive guide to managing debt and improving your credit score. Harzog provides actionable strategies for negotiating with creditors, creating a budget, and reducing debt.

"Your Money or Your Life: 9 Steps to Transforming Your Relationship with Money and Achieving Financial Independence" by Vicki Robin and Joe Dominguez - This book offers a holistic approach to managing debt and building wealth. Robin and Dominguez emphasize the importance of reducing expenses, increasing income, and developing a healthy relationship with money.

Chapter 9 Mindful Spending

Money management is not just about saving and investing. It also includes the way we spend our money. Mindful spending is an approach to spending money that encourages us to be more intentional, purposeful, and aware of our spending habits. It's a way of spending money that aligns with our values, priorities, and goals.

In this chapter, we'll explore the concept of mindful spending, how to practice it, and the benefits it can bring to our financial lives.

What is Mindful Spending?

Mindful spending is a practice that involves being aware of our spending habits and making conscious decisions about how we use our money. It's about spending our money in a way that aligns with our values, goals, and priorities.

Instead of mindlessly spending our money on things that we don't really need or want, mindful spending encourages us to be intentional and purposeful with our spending. It involves taking the time to evaluate our purchases and asking ourselves if they align with our values and priorities.

How to Practice Mindful Spending

Practicing mindful spending can take some effort and discipline, but it's a worthwhile habit to develop. Here are some tips on how to practice mindful spending:

Set Spending Priorities

The first step in practicing mindful spending is to identify your spending priorities. This involves taking the time to think about what's important to you and what you want to achieve with your money.

Do you value experiences over material possessions? Are you saving for a specific goal, like a down payment on a house or a dream vacation? Once you've identified your priorities, you can create a budget that reflects those values.

Create a Spending Plan

Creating a spending plan can help you stay on track with your mindful spending goals. It involves setting a budget for your expenses, including your monthly bills, groceries, entertainment, and other discretionary spending.

When creating a spending plan, be sure to allocate money for your spending priorities first. This will help ensure that you're spending your money in a way that aligns with your values.

Take Time Before Making Purchases

One of the hallmarks of mindful spending is taking the time to evaluate purchases before making them. Before making a purchase, ask yourself if it aligns with your spending priorities and if it's something that you really need or want.

Taking time before making a purchase can also help you avoid impulse buying and buyer's remorse.

Practice Gratitude

Practicing gratitude is an important aspect of mindful spending. When we focus on the things we're grateful for, we're less likely to feel the need to buy more things to make us happy.

Try practicing gratitude by keeping a journal or taking a few minutes each day to reflect on the things you're thankful for. This can help shift your focus away from material possessions and towards the things that truly matter in life.

The Benefits of Mindful Spending

Practicing mindful spending can bring a number of benefits to our financial lives, including:

Reduced Stress

When we practice mindful spending, we're less likely to feel the stress that comes with overspending and financial instability. We're able to stay on top of our finances and make conscious decisions about how we use our money.

Increased Savings

By being more intentional with our spending, we can also increase our savings. When we focus on our spending priorities and avoid impulse buying, we're able to put more money towards our savings goals.

Improved Relationships

Mindful spending can also improve our relationships with others. When we're not focused on material possessions, we're more likely to focus on the people in our lives and the experiences we share with them.

Greater Happiness

Finally, practicing mindful spending can lead to greater happiness.

In conclusion, spending wisely is a crucial aspect of achieving financial stability and security. By being mindful of our spending habits and making intentional choices about where our money goes, we can better control our finances and make progress towards our financial goals. It's important to remember that spending wisely doesn't mean living a life of deprivation or denying ourselves the things we enjoy. Rather, it's about finding a balance between enjoying the present moment and being responsible for our future financial wellbeing

By implementing the strategies discussed in this chapter, such as creating a budget, tracking our expenses, and being intentional about our spending, we can develop good spending habits and avoid falling into the trap of mindless consumerism. We can also work to cultivate a mindset of gratitude and contentment, focusing on the things that truly matter in life rather than constantly chasing after more material possessions.

Ultimately, spending wisely is about taking control of our finances and our lives, rather than letting our finances control us. By making mindful choices about our spending, we can build a foundation of financial stability and security that will serve us well both now and in the future.

Chapter 9 Recommended Book Resources:

(If you click on one of the links and purchase I will receive an affiliate commission)

"The 7 Habits of Highly Effective People" by Stephen R. Covey - While not specifically about spending, this book offers principles for effective living that can help you prioritize your values and make wiser choices with your money.

"Broke Millennial: Stop Scraping By and Get Your Financial Life Together" by Erin Lowry - This book offers practical advice for young adults on how to manage their money and make smarter spending decisions.

"The Art of Frugal Hedonism: A Guide to Spending Less While Enjoying Everything More" by Annie Raser-Rowland and Adam Grubb - This book challenges the idea that frugal living means sacrificing enjoyment, offering tips for how to spend less while still having a fulfilling life.

Chapter 10 Navigating Life Transitions

Life is full of changes, and transitions are an inevitable part of the human experience. Whether it's starting a new job, getting married, having children, buying a house, or going through a divorce, major life changes can bring a sense of excitement, fear, and uncertainty.

Navigating life transitions requires a unique set of skills, including adaptability, resilience, and the ability to manage stress. It also requires a thoughtful approach to managing your finances, as major life transitions can have a significant impact on your financial well-being.

In this chapter, we'll explore the challenges of navigating life transitions and provide tips and strategies for managing your finances during these times of change.

Challenges of Navigating Life Transitions

Transitions can be stressful, even when they're positive ones. Starting a new job, for example, may be exciting, but it can also be overwhelming as you navigate new responsibilities, expectations, and work relationships. On the other hand, negative transitions such as divorce or losing a job can be incredibly challenging, leaving you feeling uncertain about your future and your finances.

Financially, life transitions can be a major source of stress. Starting a new job may mean a change in income, which can impact your budget. Getting married or having children can bring new expenses and financial responsibilities. Divorce or the loss of a job can leave you struggling to make ends meet.

Whatever the transition may be, it's important to recognize the potential challenges and prepare accordingly.

Tips for Navigating Life Transitions

Plan ahead

One of the best ways to navigate life transitions is to plan ahead as much as possible. Whether you're starting a new job, getting married, or having a child, take the time to research and prepare for the transition. Create a budget that takes into account any changes in income or expenses, and think about how you can adjust your financial plan to accommodate these changes.

Communicate with your partner

If you're going through a life transition with a partner, it's important to communicate openly and honestly about your finances. Discuss your financial goals and priorities, and work together to create a budget that meets your needs. Make sure you're both on the same page about your financial expectations and responsibilities.

Seek support

Going through a major life transition can be isolating, but it's important to remember that you don't have to go through it alone. Seek support from friends, family, or a professional counselor if necessary. You may also want to consider working with a financial planner who can help you navigate the financial implications of the transition.

Be flexible

Transitions rarely go exactly as planned, and it's important to be flexible and adaptable when things don't go according to plan. If you experience a setback, don't beat yourself up over it. Instead, focus on what you can do to move forward and stay positive.

Prioritize self-care

Finally, don't forget to take care of yourself during times of transition. Stress can take a toll on your physical and emotional health, so make sure you're getting enough sleep, exercise, and healthy food. Take time to do things that bring you joy and relaxation, whether it's reading a book, taking a walk, or spending time with loved ones.

In conclusion, navigating life transitions can be a challenging but necessary process. Whether it's starting a new job, getting married, having a child, or retiring, transitions require us to adapt and adjust to new circumstances. However, with the right mindset and strategies, we can successfully navigate these transitions and come out stronger on the other side.

Remember to take time to reflect on your values and priorities, seek support from friends and family, and be open to new opportunities. By approaching life transitions with a growth mindset, we can turn them into opportunities for personal growth and transformation. Don't forget to be kind to yourself, practice self-care, and stay optimistic even during difficult times.

There will be challenges and setbacks, but by developing resilience and a positive outlook, we can overcome them and continue moving forward towards our goals. Keep learning, growing, and adapting to new situations, and you will be well-equipped to handle whatever life throws your way.

Chapter 10 Recommended Book Resources:

(If you click on one of the links and purchase I will receive an affiliate commission)

"The One-Page Financial Plan: A Simple Way to Be Smart About Your Money" by Carl Richards

"The Financial Diet: A Total Beginner's Guide to Getting Good with Money" by Chelsea Fagan and Lauren Ver Hage

"You Need a Budget: The Proven System for Breaking the Paycheck-to-Paycheck Cycle, Getting Out of Debt, and Living the Life You Want" by Jesse Mecham

In conclusion, mastering your money mind is essential to achieving financial success and freedom. Traditional financial advice often provides a cookie-cutter approach that may not work for everyone. It's time to break free from this one-size-fits-all mentality and adopt a personalized approach that aligns with your unique goals and values.

The first step is to examine your money mindset and identify any limiting beliefs or patterns that may be holding you back. From there, you can work on developing a more positive and empowering mindset that encourages smart financial decisions and habits.

Next, take a holistic approach to your finances, considering not just your income and expenses, but also your debt, savings, investments, and long-term goals. Create a personalized financial plan that prioritizes your values and aligns with your unique circumstances.

Don't be afraid to seek out expert advice and guidance when needed, but remember to be selective in choosing the right professionals to work with. Trust your gut instincts and don't be afraid to ask questions or seek out a second opinion.

Finally, remember that financial success is not just about the numbers, but also about finding joy and fulfillment in your life. Practicing mindful spending and focusing on experiences and relationships rather than material possessions can bring a sense of abundance and contentment that money alone cannot provide.

Overall, by mastering your money mind, you can break free from traditional financial advice and create a personalized approach to achieving financial success and freedom. It takes time, effort, and commitment, but the rewards are well worth it in the end.

Recommended Resources:

WRITE A BOOK IN A DAY WITH CHATGPT

If you would like to know how I wrote this book in 1 day completely using Chat GPT enroll in the following Chat GPT Mini Course Writing Content in the Blink of an Eye with Kelly Falardeau and Kimberly Crowe

https://cpnoshea--checkingout.thrivecart.com/chatgpt/

Chapter 2 Recommended Book Resources:

"The Millionaire Mind" by Thomas J. Stanley - This book explores the habits, attitudes, and beliefs of millionaires and how they differ from those of the general population.

"Think and Grow Rich" by Napoleon Hill - This classic book emphasizes the importance of positive thinking and visualization in achieving financial success.

"The Psychology of Money" by Morgan Housel - This book explores the intersection of psychology and finance and how our beliefs and behaviors around money impact our financial outcomes.

"The Power of Positive Thinking" by Norman Vincent Peale - This book focuses on the role of positive thinking and attitude in achieving success in all areas of life, including finance.

Chapter 3 Recommended Book Resources:

"The Simple Path to Wealth" by JL Collins - This book challenges traditional financial advice and promotes a simple, DIY approach to investing.

"Your Money or Your Life" by Vicki Robin and Joe Dominguez - This book offers a holistic approach to personal finance, emphasizing the importance of aligning your spending and saving habits with your values and goals

Chapter 4 Recommended Book Resources:

"Mindset: The New Psychology of Success" by Carol Dweck - This book explores the concept of fixed and growth mindsets and how they impact our ability to learn, grow, and achieve our goals.

"The Power of Now" by Eckhart Tolle - This book focuses on the importance of being present in the moment and how our thoughts and beliefs can limit our ability to experience inner peace and happiness.

"Breaking the Habit of Being Yourself: How to Lose Your Mind and Create a New One" by Joe Dispenza - This book provides insights into how the mind works and offers practical strategies for overcoming limiting beliefs and behaviors.

"The Gifts of Imperfection: Let Go of Who You Think You're Supposed to Be and Embrace Who You Are" by Brené Brown - This book encourages readers to let go of perfectionism and embrace vulnerability as a means

Atomic Habits an Easy & Proven Way to Build Good Habits and Break Bad Ones James Clear This book presents a simple, evidence-based approach to building good habits and breaking bad ones. It provides practical tips for making small changes that can lead to big results over time.

"The Power of Habit: Why We Do What We Do in Life and Business" by Charles Duhigg This book examines the science of habits and how they shape our lives, both personally and professionally. It provides actionable advice for breaking bad habits and building good ones.

Chapter 5 Recommended Book Resources:

"Your Money and Your Brain" by Jason Zweig - This book explores the connection between brain chemistry and financial decision-making, providing insights into how emotions can influence our financial choices.

"Mind Over Money: The Psychology of Money and How to Use It Better" by Claudia Hammond - This book delves into the psychology behind our financial choices and provides practical tips for managing our money and emotions.

"Emotional Agility: Get Unstuck, Embrace Change, and Thrive in Work and Life" by Susan David - Although not specifically about money, this book provides insights into how to better understand and manage our emotions in all aspects of life, which can be applied to financial decision-making.

"The Behavioral Investor" by Daniel Crosby - This book explores the intersection of psychology and finance, providing insights into the emotional and cognitive biases that can impact our financial choices.

“Money, A Love Story: Untangle Your Financial Woes and Create the Life You Really Want" by Kate Northrup - This book focuses on the emotional relationship that we have with money, and provides strategies for transforming negative money beliefs and behaviors.

Chapter 6 Recommended Book Resources

"Rich Dad Poor Dad" by Robert Kiyosaki is a personal finance book that emphasizes the importance of financial education, investing, and entrepreneurship. The author shares his personal story of growing up with two different father figures - his biological father (poor dad) and his best friend's father (rich dad). The book highlights the different financial philosophies of these two individuals and how their beliefs and actions shaped their financial outcomes.

“Cash Flow Quadrant” by Robert Kiyosaki is a follow-up book to "Rich Dad Poor Dad" and focuses on the four different ways people earn money: as employees, self-employed individuals, business owners, or investors. Kiyosaki argues that people who want to achieve financial independence need to move from the left side of the cash flow quadrant (employee or self-employed) to the right side (business owner or investor).

"The Total Money Makeover" by Dave Ramsey is a personal

finance book that provides a step-by-step plan for people to get out of debt and build wealth. The book focuses on seven "baby steps" that individuals can take to achieve financial freedom, including saving an emergency fund, paying off debt, and investing for retirement. Ramsey's approach emphasizes the importance of living below one's means and avoiding debt at all costs.

Chapter 7 Recommended Book Resources:

Start Late, Finish Rich: A No-Fail Plan for Achieving Financial Freedom at Any Age by David Bach In a swift, motivating read, David Bach gives you step-by-step instructions, worksheets, phone numbers, and website addresses—everything you need to put your "Start Late" plan into place right away. You will learn that even if you're buried in debt, there's still hope. You can spend less, save more, and make more—and it doesn't have to hurt. With America's best-loved money coach at your side, it's never too late to change your financial destiny.

"The Automatic Millionaire" by David Bach is a personal finance book that emphasizes the importance of automating one's savings and investment contributions to achieve financial independence. Bach argues that by setting up automatic contributions to retirement accounts and other investment vehicles, individuals can save and invest without having to think about it. The book also stresses the importance of living below one's means and avoiding unnecessary expenses.

"The 4-Hour Work Week" by Timothy Ferriss: This book presents a new perspective on wealth-building, focusing on lifestyle design, productivity, and entrepreneurship.

"The Richest Man in Babylon" by George S. Clason - This book offers timeless financial advice through parables set in ancient Babylon, emphasizing the importance of disciplined saving and investing.

"The ABCs of Real Estate Investing" by Ken McElroy - This book covers the basics of real estate investing, including finding deals, evaluating properties, financing, and managing rental properties.

McElroy also includes case studies and real-world examples.

"The Millionaire Real Estate Investor" by Gary Keller, Dave Jenks, and Jay Papasan - This book provides practical advice on how to become a successful real estate investor, covering topics such as finding investment properties, financing deals, and building a portfolio.

Chapter 8 Recommended Book Resources:

"Debt-Free Forever: Take Control of Your Money and Your Life" by Gail Vaz-Oxlade - This book offers practical advice for eliminating debt and creating a sustainable financial plan. Vaz-Oxlade emphasizes the importance of understanding your spending habits and making changes to live within your means.

"The Debt Escape Plan: How to Free Yourself From Credit Card Balances, Boost Your Credit Score, and Live Debt-Free" by Beverly Harzog - This book offers a comprehensive guide to managing debt and improving your credit score. Harzog provides actionable strategies for negotiating with creditors, creating a budget, and reducing debt.

"Your Money or Your Life: 9 Steps to Transforming Your Relationship with Money and Achieving Financial Independence" by Vicki Robin and Joe Dominguez - This book offers a holistic approach to managing debt and building wealth. Robin and Dominguez emphasize the importance of reducing expenses, increasing income, and developing a healthy relationship with money.

Chapter 9 Recommended Book Resources:

(If you click on one of the links and purchase I will receive an affiliate commission)

"The 7 Habits of Highly Effective People" by Stephen R. Covey - While not specifically about spending, this book offers principles for effective living that can help you prioritize your values and make wiser choices with your money.

"Broke Millennial: Stop Scraping By and Get Your Financial Life Together" by Erin Lowry - This book offers practical advice for young adults on how to manage their money and make smarter spending decisions.

"The Art of Frugal Hedonism: A Guide to Spending Less While Enjoying Everything More" by Annie Raser-Rowland and Adam Grubb - This book challenges the idea that frugal living means sacrificing enjoyment, offering tips for how to spend less while still having a fulfilling life.

Chapter 10 Recommended Book Resources:

"The One-Page Financial Plan: A Simple Way to Be Smart About Your Money" by Carl Richards

"The Financial Diet: A Total Beginner's Guide to Getting Good with Money" by Chelsea Fagan and Lauren Ver Hage

"You Need a Budget: The Proven System for Breaking the Paycheck-to-Paycheck Cycle, Getting Out of Debt, and Living the Life You Want" by Jesse Mecham

ABOUT THE AUTHOR

I am a seasoned digital marketer with over 15 years of experience in the financial industry. Throughout my career, I have developed a deep passion for helping individuals take control of their finances and achieve financial freedom. My expertise in digital marketing has enabled me to effectively communicate complex financial concepts to diverse audiences and empower them to make informed financial decisions.

As an entrepreneur and business owner myself, I understand the unique financial challenges that come with running a business. Over the years, I have developed a practical and empowering approach to money management that is tailored specifically to entrepreneurs. My goal is to help business owners achieve financial success and create a sustainable, profitable business.

When I'm not working on digital marketing strategies or helping people with their finances, I enjoy spending timewith my wife and our 5 kids, and our pets.

Are you ready to turn your passion into a profitable source of passive income?

Look no further!

With our proven system, you can earn $5,000 - $10,000 or more in commissions by writing a book and creating an audiobook. Here's how it works:

Step 1: Choose a niche that you are knowledgeable and passionate about. This will be the topic of your book.
Step 2: I will write an engaging and informative book that provides value to your target audience. I will provide you with a step-by-step guide and templates to make the writing process easy and efficient.
Step 3: Record your audiobook yourself or use our professional recording service. This will allow your audience to enjoy your book on the go and reach a wider audience.
Step 4: Promote your book using our proven marketing strategies to generate affiliate commissions. I will market your book effectively, including leveraging Facebook Ads, email marketing, and affiliate partnerships.
Step 5: Sit back and watch the passive income roll in! With ongoing support from our team, you can continue to earn recurring commissions and grow your income over time.

This is not a get-rich-quick scheme. It requires dedication, hard work, and patience. But with our system, you will have all the tools and support you need to succeed.

So, what are you waiting for? Start writing your book today and take the first step towards earning $5,000 - $10,000 in commissions in the next 60-90 days.

During this free 30-minute Passive Income Powerhouse Session, we will dive deep into your current internet marketing strategies and identify opportunities to boost your commissions.

Together, we will create a personalized action plan tailored to your unique goals and challenges, so you can start earning passive income quickly and consistently.

We will also discuss how to leverage your strengths and optimize your resources to maximize your results.

By the end of this session, you will have a clear roadmap to take your affiliate marketing game to the next level. Let's work together to turn your efforts into profits and achieve the financial freedom you deserve!

Book Your Free 30 Minute Session Now.

https://tinyurl.com/30minutepowersession

Made in United States
Troutdale, OR
11/03/2026

56852688R00030

MASTER YOUR MONEY MIND

I am a seasoned digital marketer with over 15 years of experience in the financial industry. Throughout my career, I have developed a deep passion for helping individuals take control of their finances and achieve financial freedom. My expertise in digital marketing has enabled me to effectively communicate complex financial concepts to diverse audiences and empower them to make informed financial decisions.

As an entrepreneur and business owner myself, I understand the unique financial challenges that come with running a business. Over the years, I have developed a practical and empowering approach to money management that is tailored specifically to entrepreneurs. My goal is to help business owners achieve financial success and create a sustainable, profitable business.

When I'm not working on digital marketing strategies or helping people with their finances, I enjoy spending timewith my wife and our 5 kids, and our pets.

ISBN 9781959555728

90000

9 781959 555728

CRYPTOCURRENCY INVESTING BASICS

An Introduction to Blockchain, Digital Assets, and Risk Awareness

ARKON FLUX